How To Teach Drama To Kids

Your Step By Step Guide To Teaching Drama To Kids

HowExpert with Julie Johnson

Copyright HowExpert™
www.HowExpert.com

For more tips related to this topic, visit HowExpert.com/teachdrama.

Recommended Resources

- HowExpert.com – Quick 'How To' Guides on All Topics from A to Z by Everyday Experts.
- HowExpert.com/free – Free HowExpert Email Newsletter.
- HowExpert.com/books – HowExpert Books
- HowExpert.com/courses – HowExpert Courses
- HowExpert.com/clothing – HowExpert Clothing
- HowExpert.com/membership – HowExpert Membership Site
- HowExpert.com/affiliates – HowExpert Affiliate Program
- HowExpert.com/writers – Write About Your #1 Passion/Knowledge/Expertise & Become a HowExpert Author.
- HowExpert.com/resources – Additional HowExpert Recommended Resources
- YouTube.com/HowExpert – Subscribe to HowExpert YouTube.
- Instagram.com/HowExpert – Follow HowExpert on Instagram.
- Facebook.com/HowExpert – Follow HowExpert on Facebook.

COPYRIGHT, LEGAL NOTICE AND DISCLAIMER:

COPYRIGHT © BY HOWEXPERT™ (OWNED BY HOT METHODS). ALL RIGHTS RESERVED WORLDWIDE. NO PART OF THIS PUBLICATION MAY BE REPRODUCED IN ANY FORM OR BY ANY MEANS, INCLUDING SCANNING, PHOTOCOPYING, OR OTHERWISE WITHOUT PRIOR WRITTEN PERMISSION OF THE COPYRIGHT HOLDER.

DISCLAIMER AND TERMS OF USE: PLEASE NOTE THAT MUCH OF THIS PUBLICATION IS BASED ON PERSONAL EXPERIENCE AND ANECDOTAL EVIDENCE. ALTHOUGH THE AUTHOR AND PUBLISHER HAVE MADE EVERY REASONABLE ATTEMPT TO ACHIEVE COMPLETE ACCURACY OF THE CONTENT IN THIS GUIDE, THEY ASSUME NO RESPONSIBILITY FOR ERRORS OR OMISSIONS. ALSO, YOU SHOULD USE THIS INFORMATION AS YOU SEE FIT, AND AT YOUR OWN RISK. YOUR PARTICULAR SITUATION MAY NOT BE EXACTLY SUITED TO THE EXAMPLES ILLUSTRATED HERE; IN FACT, IT'S LIKELY THAT THEY WON'T BE THE SAME, AND YOU SHOULD ADJUST YOUR USE OF THE INFORMATION AND RECOMMENDATIONS ACCORDINGLY.

THE AUTHOR AND PUBLISHER DO NOT WARRANT THE PERFORMANCE, EFFECTIVENESS OR APPLICABILITY OF ANY SITES LISTED OR LINKED TO IN THIS BOOK. ALL LINKS ARE FOR INFORMATION PURPOSES ONLY AND ARE NOT WARRANTED FOR CONTENT, ACCURACY OR ANY OTHER IMPLIED OR EXPLICIT PURPOSE.

ANY TRADEMARKS, SERVICE MARKS, PRODUCT NAMES OR NAMED FEATURES ARE ASSUMED TO BE THE PROPERTY OF THEIR RESPECTIVE OWNERS, AND ARE USED ONLY FOR REFERENCE. THERE IS NO IMPLIED ENDORSEMENT IF WE USE ONE OF THESE TERMS.

NO PART OF THIS BOOK MAY BE REPRODUCED, STORED IN A RETRIEVAL SYSTEM, OR TRANSMITTED BY ANY OTHER MEANS: ELECTRONIC, MECHANICAL, PHOTOCOPYING, RECORDING, OR OTHERWISE, WITHOUT THE PRIOR WRITTEN PERMISSION OF THE AUTHOR.

ANY VIOLATION BY STEALING THIS BOOK OR DOWNLOADING OR SHARING IT ILLEGALLY WILL BE PROSECUTED BY LAWYERS TO THE FULLEST EXTENT. THIS PUBLICATION IS PROTECTED UNDER THE US COPYRIGHT ACT OF 1976 AND ALL OTHER APPLICABLE INTERNATIONAL, FEDERAL, STATE AND LOCAL LAWS AND ALL RIGHTS ARE RESERVED, INCLUDING RESALE RIGHTS: YOU ARE NOT ALLOWED TO GIVE OR SELL THIS GUIDE TO ANYONE ELSE.

THIS PUBLICATION IS DESIGNED TO PROVIDE ACCURATE AND AUTHORITATIVE INFORMATION WITH REGARD TO THE SUBJECT MATTER COVERED. IT IS SOLD WITH THE UNDERSTANDING THAT THE AUTHORS AND PUBLISHERS ARE NOT ENGAGED IN RENDERING LEGAL, FINANCIAL, OR OTHER PROFESSIONAL ADVICE. LAWS AND PRACTICES OFTEN VARY FROM STATE TO STATE AND IF LEGAL OR OTHER EXPERT ASSISTANCE IS REQUIRED, THE SERVICES OF A PROFESSIONAL SHOULD BE SOUGHT. THE AUTHORS AND PUBLISHER SPECIFICALLY DISCLAIM ANY LIABILITY THAT IS INCURRED FROM THE USE OR APPLICATION OF THE CONTENTS OF THIS BOOK.

COPYRIGHT BY HOWEXPERT™ (OWNED BY HOT METHODS)
ALL RIGHTS RESERVED WORLDWIDE.

Table of Contents

Recommended Resources 2
Introduction to Teaching Drama to Young People 6
Chapter 1: Movement Exercises and Tips 9
   Introduction to Movement 9
      Warm – Up #1: Statues 10
      Warm Up # 2 10
      Exercises: 11
   TIPS FOR THE TEACHER: 17
      Negative Points to Watch Out For: 17
      Positive Points to Suggest: 18
   TIPS FOR THE TEACHER: 20
Chapter 2: Voice Exercises and Tips 22
   Introduction to Voice Exercises 22
      Exercise #1: Tossing the Ball 24
      Exercise # 2: The Telephone Game 25
      Exercise # 3 - MY Home Town 27
      Exercise #4 - Tongue Twisters 28
      Exercise # 5: Practicing Variances in Inflection 29
   TIP FOR THE TEACHER: 31
Chapter 3: Improvisational Exercises and Tips 33
   Introduction to Improvisation 33
Chapter 4: Storytelling and Early Characterization
Exercises 53
   Introduction to Storytelling and Characters 53
      Storytelling with CHARACTERS - Demo And
      Intro For All Three Groups 54
   TIPS FOR THE TEACHER: 64
Chapter 5: Puppetry Exercises and Tips 65
   Introduction to Puppetry 65

Chapter 6: Early Stage Conflict and Fight Scenes 79
　Introduction to Dramatic Physical Conflicts 79
　Slaps, Punches, and Push/Pulls 82
　　Teaching A Stage Slap 84
　The Stage Punch 85
　Push/Pulls 86
　TIPS FOR THE TEACHER: 88
Chapter 7: Clowning and Mask Exercises and Tips ..90
　Introduction to Clowning and Masks 90
　　Exercise #1: The Study...95
　　Exercise #2: (to take place ONLY after Exercise #1 has been completed satisfactorily in several different sets/pairs.) 96
Chapter 8: Choreographed Steps and Simple Chorus Line Work..101
　Introduction to Chorus Line Stepping/Dance......101
　TIPS FOR THE TEACHER: 105
Chapter 9: Scene Work and Skits 107
　Introduction to Scene Work 107
　　Exercise #1 for All Groups 107
　　Group One: Scenes for the Younger Children ..109
　　Group Two: Some Suggested Scenes for the Pre-Teens 109
　TIPS FOR THE TEACHER: 110
Glossary of Basic Theater Terms Used in this Text..112
About the Expert 117
Recommended Resources..118

Introduction to Teaching Drama to Young People

Though I'm a high school drama teacher now, years ago, when asked to lead my very first workshop, I was still in teacher's college and the workshop was for 22 adults – some from an amateur "Players" local, some senior citizens from a group called "Sage Age Theater." They requested a day-long affair, with a general theme, so therefore exercises in every aspect. How, I wondered, would I keep everyone busy and interested? How, though I'd been on stage for years myself, would I TEACH these people what I knew?

Of course, now I look back fondly on that first-ever workshop. It had all gone so smoothly, everyone (even the hard-of-hearing seniors) listening intently as though I were MOSES passing on the Commandments, every student taking seriously each exercise I introduced, practicing each diligently, whether I was there hovering over them or elsewhere across the room.

I've never since then taught a drama workshop or lesson so "text-book perfect," and NEITHER WILL YOU, if you're teaching under 20-year-olds. You'll have no end of surprises, some amusing, some frustrating. You'll have to think on your feet, be flexible, add exercises here, adjust them there, or eliminate some altogether. (You may have planned for hours for one particular favourite exercise of yours – but if it isn't going to work with that group – FORGET IT. Lament later, but DO NOT TRY AND INTRODUCE IT if your instinct tells you it just isn't going to go over).

You'll need to repeat instructions many, many times, demonstrate, either using yourself or another student, be patient if none of your corrections are implemented, and most of all you'll have to remain calm while still appearing up-beat, motivated and inspired!

My first year of teaching was in an inner-city school in England, where I had 33-38 students in a class, and most classes were of children ages 10 to 12 who wanted nothing LESS than to take Drama. In the U.K. at this time, it was a mandatory course at these ages. No matter what I did that year, right from the standard sitting-on-the-floor in a "theater circle" at the beginning of each lesson, students were climbing the curtains, hiding BEHIND the curtains, grabbing props and stabbing each other, wrestling on the floor, knocking over sets built for the senior classes, etc. (This was also before chocolate and soda pops were removed from the machines in the cafeterias!)

However, many years later, though not CONSIDERABLY any different, my drama classes with children flow a little more smoothly due to the many "tricks" I've discovered, mostly through trial and error. I will share those tricks here with you, as well as many of the exercises I've found or developed which work best for various ages – and with the simplest of props, equipment and etc.

This book is designed specifically for the teaching of Theater Arts to young people. Obviously, if you are teaching a workshop to adults or a mix of ages, many of these exercises can be adapted to be equally effective. Each chapter has exercises for:

- Group One, which I suggest as being 5 to 9 year olds
- Group Two, which could be 10 to 13 year olds

and

- Group Three, which should be the more mature 14 to 18 year-olds.

You do not necessarily need to follow the order I have set out here, or obviously, to try and do EVERY component (I have even suggested that you may want to leave out teaching Stage Fighting, Mime, and Clowning and Masks). However, I have tried to set these out in a progressive order that would best suit both a workshop situation, a winter session of evening classes once or twice a week, or an entire year of classes at school. (Obviously, you'd have to add exercises and projects to each unit if the latter were the case.)

I wish you luck as you embark upon our shared goal of keeping the performing arts alive and flourishing, by introducing the subject at an early age and instilling the joys and passion to our youth, who may then go on to do the same for other generations.

Chapter 1: Movement Exercises and Tips

Introduction to Movement

To live is to breathe, to stretch, to move

To prance across wide open spaces

To gesture with fingers, hands, or arms

To spin dizzily on grassy green places

Movement is joy, or movement shows sorrow

Movement is how we express

On stage, it shows more than our lines or our faces

Much more than our stature or dress.

As discussed in the Movement Intro, above, this is one of the most freeing and potentially relaxing categories of Drama Lessons. Warm ups can include anything from Statues (a reminder of this old classic game is below), to Simon Says to some form of Follow the Leader Parade (preferably to a type of marching music)– even for Group 3, these can often work well.

WARM – UP #1: STATUES

(For many other categories such as improv and characterization exercises, Statues can also work well, with some adjustments to the relevant section.)

Choose a "buyer," who goes out of the room. Take each of the remaining students firmly by the arm and swing them round and round until they are dizzy, then "fling" them (not hard – lawsuits are always pending...!!!) into a position. They must stop and hold this position.

The "buyer" then enters, and you show them each of the "statues," pressing a "button" or pulling a "cord" on each to get them activated. Each statue must then do a performance in movement for the buyer, BASED ON THEIR ORIGINAL HELD POSITION, and after several moments, going BACK into their original held position. After the buyer has seen each, he or she may choose a statue to "buy." (You can leave this last bit out if you don't wish to make it a win/lose competition type of exercise, of course!)

WARM UP # 2

Another warm-up common for movement lessons is to have everyone move around the room separately from each other, and call out changes like:

- You're now walking in a room full of plastic balls
- You're now on a sheet of ice!
- You have diarrhea and are about to lose control of your bowels!
- The room is a frozen meat locker and you've been in here for an hour!
- The odor in this room is noxious and disgusting!
- You have a helium balloon between your knees!
- This room is in the tropics, hot and humid and you're trying to move through a jungle of vines and poisonous snakes...
- The people next to you are all carrying concealed weapons like guns and knives!
- You are walking across a very muddy field to the other side!
- You are in the desert after 4 hours of being lost (rather than suggest they crawl here, it is interesting to watch and see how many do it of their own accord!)

EXERCISES:

Group One: Waving the Caterpillar and More

An excellent movement exercise for group one is to have a series of a great variety of short music excerpts (about 15 seconds each) ready to play. Turn off the lights (makes them feel less self-conscious) and have them begin first by lying on the floor. They must "dance" on the floor to the various tunes. Then have them stand and do the same. (Encourage them not to copy each other but to do their own). Then, YOU pick groups of three or four (never a good idea to have pairs in any exercise if you can help it, and always best if YOU pick the groups, thus no one feels left out and the students are always working with different people, not always their "best friends", and have the groups hold hands, link arms, or "connect" however they like and once again, dance in rhythm to the tunes.

Lastly, the whole class should somehow "link" together physically and become a machine – this could be everyone moving the same way at the same time, or all different movements and go along like a caterpillar or "the Wave."

If your group seem to excel at this exercise, it may be possible to introduce the movement exercises for Groups Two and Three as well, with, perhaps, some simplified adjustments.

Group Two:

This exercise and the Group Three one could be used interchangeably, as both require a certain amount of maturity and self-confidence.

Dance/ Drama Sticks

I have found that bamboo sticks from the garden center, of lengths about 3 feet long are best for this exercise, although I have also used ½ inch dowels of the same length (the latter tend to be a little too heavy, however, and certainly more expensive).

Put the group in pairs (one of the few exercises where pairs, and not a larger group, are a necessity) of similar heights. This will NOT work well if one child is considerably taller than the other. Play music of a longer variety than the above excerpts, but not whole songs either. About 45 seconds each, with a good variety of speeds and rhythms. Each student will place their first finger ONLY on the end of the stick/pole. They must carefully watch each other's eyes and follow the movement of the stick up and down, as one moves high, low, around, etc. When they get really good, they can try stepping over it, going under it (spinning it on their finger end, but NEVER grasping it with one hand).

- First, or index finger, gets put on one end of stick.
- Other partner does the same.
- This can be done either by placing the stick on the floor, or by one student holding it until both partners' index fingers are in position.
- Have students try a vertical twist first, where one either bends or goes right down to the floor.
- Then have them play with horizontal lines, up high, down low...
- Have your pairs try going under and over the stick, with legs, with full body, etc. Students should not drop the stick!

If you wish to make a competition out of it, see how many daring moves the pairs can make in time to the music, without dropping the stick, or count the amount of times each pair drops it, and award the team with the least drops, who is still most matching the rhythm.

If you wish, you may then have them switch pairs.

Group Three: 3 Poses

If this exercise is taken seriously, it's one of my favorites, both to execute and to teach. Have a piece of primarily instrumental music chosen with a dramatic beginning and ending, of about 2 minutes in length (if you have a very big room) or 1 minute if only a medium sized space. To be perfect, the music should have some crescendos, diminuendos, and a change in rhythm or speed, but this is tricky to find all in a 2 minute interval. What I've done is had three different pieces and I choose ONE, depending on the size of the room: One is one minute, another is one and a half seconds, and the final excerpt is two minutes, edited by a professional so that each of them SOUNDS like they are all one unified piece within itself but with the required beginnings, endings and shifts of tempo and decibel level, etc. in each. Some good examples to look for or download are:

- Movie or Musical Overtures (work well as they have already amalgamated several "tunes" in one).
- Instrumental refrains from Stealing Home movie with Jodie Foster and Mark Harmon.
- Carnival of the Animal or Boston Pops type

recordings.
- Peter and the Wolf.
- Supertramp – certain songs from this group have wonderful dramatic excerpts either in the middle, or at the end that work beautifully.

First, have the group spread out all around the room, using every possible corner. They should not be within an arm's length of anyone else.

Next, instruct them to "pose" – any dramatic pose will do, either upright, sitting, or on the floor. Remind them to always be original – no copying others! They must remember exactly where they were for this pose, and remember the exact pose. No changing will be allowed.

Then tell them to go all the way to the other side of the room and strike another pose. It should be obviously very different and at a different level from the pose prior.

Lastly, tell them to go as far away from this last pose as they can get, and to strike and remember their LAST AND FINAL pose. Reiterate that they MUST remember where all three poses were, and what each one looked like.

Then have them all come back and sit them on the floor to listen to the music. This will be their only chance to carefully examine the swells and tempo and overall timing so they must listen carefully. But don't fully explain the exercise until AFTER they've listened, which makes it more free-flowing and less planned.

- Do have students try and come up with as many interesting and dynamic poses as possible. Just standing, or just sitting in the corner should NOT be allowed!

Once they've listened to the edited excerpt, explain that:

1. You will turn off the lights to make the room comfortable and make them feel less self-conscious. (If it's a windowless room, crack open a doorway to a lit hall, or wherever, or have a small lamp for your own use. Obviously, the room can't be PITCH black!)
2. They will get in position 1, the music will start, and they should hold the pose for as long as they feel is right (no moving just because others are...)
3. When they feel the moment is right based on their pose, their own sense of rhythm and timing, and the music itself, they should MOVE across the room toward position 2, IN TIME TO THE MUSIC, and with whatever flairs, gestures, etc. it will take to help them ease naturally from FIRST POSE TO SECOND.
4. They get in to and hold position 2 and then follow the same instructions to position 3, but should be arriving and posing here, just as the music is about to end (i.e.: they will either get in this position EXACTLY as the music ends, or should only be holding it for a matter of seconds before it finishes).

No walking or running normally. Only movement with the music is allowed, though it does not have to be a dance-like movement per se; I've seen some very slap-stick boys skip a pretend rope across the floor once across, then hop like a bunny in the next "cross."

No rushing at the end like one would do for musical chairs! And they MUST be in the same spot for their same pose all three times.

If this exercise looked sloppy and not at all what you were hoping for, then obviously you should allow them to re-do it. But, the group that can, for the most part, pull this off the very first time, is indeed a most talented bunch!

TIPS FOR THE TEACHER:

Just in case time is NOT a constraint, these are some tips to either teach to the class as a short theory lesson OR are points you should at least be watching for when coaching any of the following exercise in this book or helping to BLOCK a scene.

NEGATIVE POINTS TO WATCH OUT FOR:

- Be aware if a student is covering their face with their hands or a prop like a book (this will garble or muffle the sound and prevent facial expression from being seen).
- If a line being delivered is EXTREMELY important (forwards plot, adds to conflict, or is very funny) the actor should NOT move (or CROSS) on it.

- Unless it's in the character of the role being played, a student should not cross knees or feet (awkward, and does not help voice projection).
- Unless it's in the character of the role being portrayed, an actor should never grab the arms of a chair to push themselves up.
- Do not upstage another actor. As "upstage" is the section furthest from the audience (see glossary – so called because historically the STAGE sloped from low to high for audience viewing as opposed to now when the audience 'slopes' or rises. So any student who stands further back to deliver lines, and then stays there while others turn to face him/her (thus putting their BACKS to the audience) is UPSTAGING. (Throughout this book, several comments are made about young people who FIGURATIVELY upstage others by demanding attention and "spotlight time." This is more about LITERALLY upstaging others – often unintentionally. However, you can see where the phrase has come from.
- Likewise, and this should go without saying, make sure a student is never MASKING (standing in front of) another so that the audience can not clearly see or hear that person.

POSITIVE POINTS TO SUGGEST:

- Students downstage moving up should move forward when about to make a stage cross WITH THE UPSTAGE FOOT FIRST. This is best for balance, and doesn't look awkward to the audience. When an

ENTRANCE is being made, the upstage foot should come first so that the body is turned downstage toward the audience.
- Always have students "feel" the edge of a chair or sofa with the back calf of their leg before sitting and don't let them double in half to sit or re-stand: upper body should be upright at all times.
- When kneeling, or stooping, the same should be considered: the student should keep the upper body upright as much as possible (audience can't see face if bent over, and also it appears awkward – even if it's REALLY more awkward NOT to bend forward!).
- Always have actors cross UPSTAGE of seated characters so as not to walk in front of them.
- When only two students are on stage at a time and one actor makes a cross movement clear across the stage, the other actor should COUNTER-CROSS (with some sort of REASON/PURPOSE, called "motivation") to offset the movement, better balance the stage distribution, and to avoid being blocked or upstaged by the other's new position.
- It is fine, however, to cross downstage of furniture OR characters who are standing.
- A rule-of-thumb is to have students learn to open doors using the hand nearest the hinges, and to close it with the other hand.
- And, one of my personal favorites on which to harp: ALWAYS, ALWAYS make sure students make gestures with their

UPSTAGE arm or hand (see section on slapping) so that their face is never covered, or their words muffled.
- Lastly, DO make sure actors STAY IN CHARACTER when making an exit until they are well out of sight of the audience. (Young people especially are often so thrilled to have pulled off their lines or movements in a scene, they will practically do a victory dance before they are even off the stage.)

TIPS FOR THE TEACHER:

If possible, have children always dress in tights or snug-fitting sweats, both top and bottom. Serious drama students will generally wear black as

a) exercises and sitting in theatre circle are often done on the floor or stage proper and

b) it's good practice for any work BACK or OFFSTAGE (or just out of a spotlight). They will not be seen, if they aren't supposed to be. It is also a wonderful neutral color for onstage ENSEMBLE work, where no one in particular is supposed to stand out (see comments on UPSTAGING). For chapters such as this one, in Movement, and also Physical Conflict and Chorus Line Steps, the tights – at LEAST on the bottom- are imperative. (See photos at beginning of Chorus Line Dancing chapter.)

Another tip to teach right away, and thus perfect for the Movement component, is that, while much of your exercises are hopefully done in a large room on a large floor, if the student can get a chance to "feel" the stage, it is something of an awesome procedure. Have them, only in three at a time or so, run around the stage with arms outstretched, then have them twirl around and around in the space and lastly to walk with eyes shut, or blindfolded so that they have taken comfortable 'ownership' of this space. Stand below the stage at the very front of it (below the APRON) and ensure that no one will dizzily spin right off! Other students can help you by doing this also. Often small stages must use space RIGHT up to the edge, where flaming footlights would have once made it an obvious boundary. So in modern times (see photo below) young people must experiment with as much quick movement as possible while always being very aware of how close they are to taking a tumble.

- Make sure all your students, if using the stage for any exercises or presentations, have had a chance to do the above exercises, including spinning over the stage, exploring it with eyes shut, etc. Students MUST ensure that though they work very close to the edge, right on the apron of the stage at times, they must know NOT to step that final inch or so!

Chapter 2: Voice Exercises and Tips

Introduction to Voice Exercises

The voice is the instrument most coddled

By actors on stage and on screen

It's soft or it's loud, comes from head or deep down

Almost as far down as the spleen!

Projection, and elocution, enun-and-pronun-ciation

All are essential in every day life.

For all of us, to learn to speak well

Is how communication causes less strife.

Most kids will NOT wish to spend much time concentrating on this area – it's too much like work, and they "don't see the point." So, I have only suggested here a few SHORT exercises and lessons and can be done by any age group. I will also try not to bog you down with theory about voice projection and quality. But, like I've said in the rhyming introduction, proper communication and use of the voice is so important that human resources and personnel directors say they are one of the top three assets needed for staff such as managers, supervisors or anyone who will be in the public eye. And as for an actor's voice – well, have you ever sat in the audience of a show, or watched a movie or sit-com where you missed something and desperately wished you'd known what was said?

The most important thing for any beginning actor to learn is that our voices do not correctly come from our throat (voice box) or somewhere in the top of our head, but way down in our diaphragms (and yes, if you're teaching teens you'll have to ignore all the giggles and meeting of eyes the first few times you say the word diaphragm). Have every child touch their diaphragm, then push IN as they emit a loud WWWWWHHHHOOOOOOOOP sound. Then have them pant like a dog. They can say "ha-ha-ha" as they pant. They will feel their diaphragm go in and out (see photos).

- *Touching the diaphragm to feel for "where voice should really come from..".*
- Each student should push their first and second fingers IN to their diaphragm (just below rib cage, immediate center) as they pant like a dog, emit hahahahaha, etc.

Have each student, standing, keep their head tilted up and drop their jaws in a wide stretch. They should then say "Awwwwwwwwww," and drop their jaws DOWN into their chests. This quickly confirms for them that they can't properly speak if their heads are down and their jaws don't have full movement. (see photo).

Next, have them "smile" with their eyes (see photo) and as much of their mouths as possible while doing the "Awwwwwwwwwwwwww." They will also see that any type of facial gesture being conveyed can also interfere with their voice projection. Have them then tap their larynx with the fingers while emitting sounds, so that they experiment with how their voice can be easily affected. Thus, re-iterate the importance of learning to control the voice, first in the BEST possible position (full front –see glossary- head up, relaxed, no emotion) and then moving on to the "trickier bits.")

- *Practicing any voice exercise should only be done with proper position of neck, jaw and head tilt. Make the student be in the 'jaw-crush' position, with head tilted slightly too low and thus the neck and chin can have maximum voice quality.*
- *This is the "smiling" exercise, with both eyes and mouth, experimenting to learn how facial expression and emotion can change the tonal quality of voice, as well as enunciation.*
- *In this final stage, the student experiments with tapping their larynx (voice box), and throat to adjust their voice carrying and enunciation sounds.*

EXERCISE #1: TOSSING THE BALL

Students line up facing a wall. Each should have their own 'space', preferably at least a 3 to 5 foot radius. You tell students as you go along what sounds, words or phrases you want them to be calling out. (eg. Vowel sounds, 'Hey!', 'You, there!', 'Whatcha doin'?', etc.) Start with the monosyllables.

Students must pretend they are throwing a ball against the wall at the exact second they emit the sounds. Also, at the same second, they should bounce hard on their heels. (Thus, the 'start position' would be standing on toes, with a 'ball' cupped in their hand, ready to throw it under-handed toward the wall.) As they call out "Oh!" or whatever you instruct, they bang down on their heels and toss the ball.

The purpose of this is to have them learn to "throw" their voice out, feeling it ricochet back at them, and ensuring it comes from the diaphragm as they bounce down, forcing it or "PUSHING" it up and out.

Children should do each sound, word or phrase several times each, before you call out the next one to practice. They should not pay attention to those around them, just "tossing" whenever they are "ready" (i.e.: not everyone will be calling out at the same exact time; it's more important that they have careful preparation to get the full benefit.)

EXERCISE # 2: THE TELEPHONE GAME

Assuming everyone has played this at some time or another in their lives, I won't go into much detail here. Suffice it to say that all age groups seem to enjoy this, and it's thus one of the few voice exercises that is more like a "game."

Sit in theater circle. You choose any regular, fairly long sentence to pass around the room by whispering one ear to another. If you have a large group (more than 12), it's best to start one sentence going one way, and one going the other, so that kids don't lose interest long before the sentence gets passed to them.

Remember, they can only say it ONCE each. No repeating. The whole point, of course, is that when the sentence gets around to the last person it is either complete gobble-dee-gook, or is at least very unlike what you started with. This teaches ENUNCIATION and vocal projection even at a whisper level, as well as concentration and some memory work.

- *When playing the Telephone Game (some people call it Rumors"), do make sure no "neighbors" hear the whispered line – ONLY the person to whom the line is being whispered should hear, until THEY pass it on.*

The best one I've ever had come out of a workshop was the following:

I started with the sentence "The camel came over the desert with two humps full of water and a green-wrapped parcel of glittering gold."

When it was passed all around the circle, the girl next to me was asked to repeat what she'd just heard, and she said, quite confidently: "Jane ate her dessert of lumpy water and a green piece of bread with mould."

EXERCISE # 3 - MY HOME TOWN

This is another exercise that can only be done in pairs, and as I don't particularly like pairs in drama (or phys. ed!) I don't do it very often, unless the group I have are mature enough not to have people feel left out, and are prepared to get "intimate" with someone NOT their best friend. Again, I would normally choose the pairs. If you have an odd number, you also can't do this, because you as leader/teacher MUST be available to go around the room and listen, thus you can not pair up with someone yourself.

Have the pairs lie on the floor on their backs, right ear to right ear.

(Or left to left, it doesn't matter.) Thus, their heads are quite close together, feet extended in opposite directions.

One person says a line about their home town like "In my home town, the library is made of red brick." Their partner repeats this. Each person must speak softly, but clearly and distinctly. They should be relaxed (lying down) and should be aware of their breathing, which should be regular. Then the partner says something about THEIR hometown like "in my home town there is a picnic place by the waterfalls," which is then repeated by the first person. You will go around the room listening from above, making sure you can clearly and distinctly hear each sentence being relayed.

- *Have the pairs lie on the floor on their backs, right ear to right ear.*
- *(Or left to left, it doesn't matter.) Thus, their heads are quite close together, feet extended in opposite directions. In the above photograph, the children are lying too far away from each other.*
- *If you can manage to convince them to lie with their ears almost teaching, that would be the ideal for this "Home Town" exercise.*

In the next step, everyone stands in theater circle. Go around the circle, with each person saying four things about their partner's home town to the entire class, ensuring that though they are talking and not shouting, everyone even across the circle is hearing. So, for example: "In my partner's hometown, the library is red brick, there is a pretty picnic spot, the firemen are very good-looking and there are a lot of loose dogs." This is not like the memory game; they don't have to use exact words or phrases from what their partner said. We are only interested in having a distinction between learning to enunciate in a quiet, relaxed manner with a soft voice, or enunciating with voice projection from the diaphragm in an upright position.

EXERCISE #4 - TONGUE TWISTERS

As a warm-up, have everyone try to touch their tongues to their noses and to the bottoms of their chins several times. Then have them flick their tongues from side to side to the corners of their mouths.

Have everyone (standing) repeat after you, first the most basic easiest old tongue twisters: She Sells Sea Shells, Mares Eat Oats and Does Eat Oats, Peter Piper Picked, and etc. I have a great children's recording called Silly Songs which I play for a laugh and for some audio education first. They can hear how well really good actors can do this. I also usually play the second part (the faster bit) of I Am A Very Model of a Modern Major General from Pirates of Penzance, which puts them in awe.

I have written several tongue twisters over the years which you may also wish to use:

Diane Dipstick doubts the daring duo dare to double dismount.

Gregory Gary Garrison gargled grinning as he caught the cat creeping cautiously.

Where whirlwinds whirl 'round one really wonders why whippoorwills are wary.

*E*XERCISE # 5: *P*RACTICING *V*ARIANCES IN *I*NFLECTION

Have your group try each of these, either together, to each other, or one at a time around the circle:

Say

"It was you!" (with exclamation, and emphasis on "you"),

"It was you?" (as a question, with rising inflection),

"What's the use?" with falling inflection, emphasis on 'what's),

"She is SOOO grateful" (emphasis on 'so', but don't swallow last word),

"LOOK at those FLAMES" (emphasis on first AND last words).

    I once had the first line of an impressive and memorable symbolic play, "Impromptu" by Tad Mosel, which I performed many times over the course of a two year period, including for several Drama Festivals. Every time I said the first line, I tried to change the inflection slightly to mean different things, and to put across different subtleties of my character. The line was "Well, we're here. Somebody say something."

    Mosel wrote the line with no emphasis on any of the words. I think, after two years, I had come up with at least 15 completely different ways and meanings. It caused me (and sometimes my fellow cast-mates, who were often taken aback at the changes in inflection) a great deal of frustration at times. See how many varieties your class can come up with, and have them tell you what each says about the character, or her emotions at the time she says the line.

TIP FOR THE TEACHER:

Some groups may want to sing in this Voice component – either together as a group or as a solo. Singing clearly with proper rhythm, pitch, tonality and enunciation is, of course, much more difficult, but if you're prepared to add some music for this, auditions will often include a request for a solo (whether the planned show is a musical or NOT!) so there is certainly no harm in introducing it!

A note about accents: Don't encourage them! At these ages, kids LOVE to show off with their repertoire of bad Cockney, un-P.C.ish sing-songy Indian and etc. Occasionally, you'll find someone has an excellent ear for accents and is producing very real –sounding work. However, you may have to take them aside and discourage them at this level. Reasons are: a) adjudicators and or examiners will ALWAYS mark someone down at this age; they expect you to pull off, for instance, a Blanche in Streetcar, with perhaps a soft lilt, but not a clichéd southern-belle voice.

b) the GOOD student of accents is just going to encourage the others who can NOT do it, and may even hurt someone's feelings in the group, if they are from that particular ethnicity.

Note: Political Correctness on Stage and Screen - Gone are the days of hiring a Caucasian to play a native American, and having their faces and arms painted reddish-brown, and having them step up and say "How! Me thinkums little squaw should ride with me." Now we are slightly more advanced (hopefully) we actually HIRE Natives and have them speak in their own language, or at least in English with their OWN accents. (See also section on characterization.)

Chapter 3: Improvisational Exercises and Tips

Introduction to Improvisation

Improvisational Skills are a must

Not just for when lines get flubbed

But for "speech and debate" or a comedy club

Or when political lawyers get dubbed.

It's always important to think on your feet

For jobs from business to con-men alike

Practice makes perfect, it's easy with time

So - just step on up to the mic!

Improvisation, as it says in the intro above, is considered, especially by parents who might be bringing their children to you for lessons, VERY important. It helps all of us with confidence-building and self-esteem, with speediness of thought and the elimination of redundancy. I once had an EXTREMELY shy Grade 10 student, a native American on a reservation in Montana. He didn't wish to speak in class at ALL – ever. I asked him to come after school with two others – Grade 9 students. First of all, it helped Jessup* so much that he was the eldest. Secondly, there were, of course fewer people in the room. We worked on some of the exercises in this chapter – which most consider fun anyway. We had two more meetings after school in the following weeks, and finally Jessup started to speak in the exercises in his own Drama classes. He began to enjoy the challenge of thinking quickly, or of speaking when no one else could think of anything relevant to say. Two years later, at his graduation, Jessup had one of the highest average marks in his Grade 12 class, and today he is a lawyer, representing primarily other Native Americans who struggle to have their own voices heard.

Most people, and especially young people, are very reluctant to get up in front of others and speak without having anything planned to say ahead of time.

For Group 1, Statues is again another excellent warm-up for improv. Then, I suggest the following for all three groups as a warm-up. If possible, set them up with a mic stand (or a self-standing lamp without the shade and bulb) and/or a spot-light/floodlight (or I often used the overhead projector) to shine on them. This helps them a) take the exercise more seriously, b) feel more in control over the others, and c) not SEE the others, so they feel it is more like they are talking to a black space.

You sit near them – about ten or fifteen feet away, facing slightly out (so they are "sharing" the audience with you) and facing slightly toward them. Ask them to answer your questions – personal questions about themselves, their pets, their holidays, their hobbies. Ask the students DIFFERENT questions, so those in the audience are not sitting out there PLANNING.

They need to answer in a minimum of three sentences each, facing out toward the audience. Go through each student until all have spoken, then you are ready, whether in this lesson (workshop situation) or the next (school situation) for the main improv. exercises, divided into age groups below:

Group One: Funny "Fill in the Blanks" Limericks

This can also be done as a warm-up, and can be done with the whole group, shouting out, or going around the circle with each taking a turn. If you're good at limericks (aabba) or just an abcb rhyme scheme, write your own about members of the class, which they heartily enjoy! You MAY need to explain the rhyme scheme first (some learning disabilities, for instance, definitely won't catch on right away, but otherwise, most students will grasp the format quickly).

Read the following (which I wrote for this particular exercise as it gets progressively more difficult) out loud, and when you come to a blank, draw a line in the air, and wait for the 'correct' word.

There once was a boy named Tony

Who rode to school on a _____

She was a fat mare

But the boy didn't care!

He was not a snob or a phony.

Now Tony had not done his homework

And he really felt like a jerk

He could not learn to add

And Teacher'd be _____

And the rest of the students would smirk.

When he got to school he sat down

And looked very sad, with a frown

The teacher said "hey!"

What's the matter today?"

And Tony smiled wide, like a
_____.

For Tony thought Teacher was kind

She was pretty and had such a smart
_____.

When she wrote on the board

Tony prayed "Oh, Dear _____,"

Make Teacher not know I'm behind…"

But Teacher wrote nineteen plus two

And then turned and paused for a few

Then "Tony, you go –

For I'm sure that you _____

You won't even need a _____!"

Poor Tony looked up from his lap

Then stood and on his head, put his
_____

He said "Teacher, my horse

Is in the stable, of _____

And my work's in my saddleflap!"

So out went the bar to the barn.

And as he walked, he said "Gosh, Golly, _____!

Teacher's upset

But I'm still Teacher's _____"

-----And that's the end of this silly yarn.

Group Two: At My Party

Divide the children into groups of four or five. One student is the party host. Give the other children a "personality" they are to act out with character-driven words and phrases, without actually saying what/who they are to the host.

Examples are:

- A homeless hobo who travels from town to town.
- A slimy fish who blows bubbles and can't find the lake.
- An alien who is studying the human race.
- A telephone operator who hates her job.
- A nasty troll who lives under a bridge.
- A giraffe with a stiff neck/sore throat.
- A woman obsessed with only dating carnival workers or circus performers.

- A forgetful man with a metal plate in his head which attracts magnetic forces.
- A toy soldier afraid of Christmas Eve in case he's given to a nasty child.
- A bad stand-up comic who tries constantly to make everyone laugh.
- Any popular cartoon character familiar to all the kids.

Each student comes to the door separately. The host welcomes them to his/her "house," offering a place to sit, offering to take "coat" – or skin, or whatever, offering drinks and food, etc., all the while trying to question and figure out by the answers what each guest is. Let each new "guest" have several moments before the doorbell rings again. Once all the guests have "arrived," they should spend several minutes interacting in character with each other, not just the host/hostess. At the end of the "party" (your call as to when), the host must try and decide what or who each of his/her guests was.

Group Three:

If this age group are very mature and serious about the study of drama, you may want to use the following as another improvisational warm up instead of some of the above.

Mature Student Warm-Up

Each person is given a short paragraph, on which you pencil in their name at the top (retype from any book, but make sure the words you eliminate are fairly obvious or at least could have several "answers" that make sense). Each student is given one minute, 30 seconds to quietly read over their paragraph and decide how to fill in each blank. THEN RECOLLECT THE PARAGRAPHS. (This is so they can't sit in the "audience" and have more time to work out their blank words. You'd think you could just tell them to turn the paper over on the floor in front of them, but a) kids can read through paper and b) they will often flip them over when you're not looking.)

You can either set the paragraph up with SOME clues at the bottom for them such as:

"Both movers were really red-faced and

1 by the time they got the

2 downstairs. I followed them as they

3 it across the living

4 , then through the dining room. Mom came out of the kitchen, her

5 jammed into her jeans pockets, and watched from the doorway as they rolled the

6 with the

2 into the family room.

1	is a descriptive adjective
2	is something heavy
3	is a verb with "ed" on the end as a suffix
4	is a noun
5	is a body part
6	is something movers use

OR

Just use a paragraph set up like this:

When _____ goes into the woods, he brings his _____, his easel, and a big canvas. When I go into the _____ with him, I bring a _____, jar, and some shortbread. We _____ the shortbread. My dad has been all over the _____ looking for just the right _____ painting. He likes oak _____, shadows, _____ and water. I have been all over the woods looking for a unicorn _____, a sphinx caterpillar, and a green _____ frog, because my interest lies less in the _____ and more in myth and biology.

    Whatever way you choose to hand out papers with these paragraphs, continue to stipulate that only ONE word should be applied to each blank AND that the paragraph must make sense.

After their one minute, thirty seconds, each student goes up to the front and reads aloud, filling in their blanks as they go along.

Group Three

Warm-Up

I have a box of a variety of items that most young people today don't recognize. (The fact that I collect primitive kitchen utensils and tools is certainly a help here, but use your imagination to make your own collection – see photos for some ideas – even PART of something else that your teens won't recognize would work well, as long as it isn't OBVIOUSLY only a "part.")

While I don't usually like to introduce anything in the grab bag that is breakable, this odd "joke" object is often too good NOT to use!

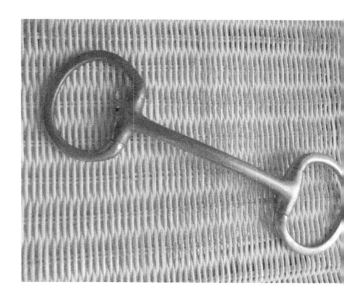

Unless you have someone in your group who rides (and thus will instantly recognize these items and thus ruin if for everyone,) there are any number of strange and unusual bits, stirrups irons, etc. from an equestrian's shelves which prove most useful in this exercise.

Antiques of a variety of sorts and materials which seem unusual are excellent choices. While I have many brasses with dogs or horses, it's best to use a less-obvious and more suggestive to all ideas type of harness decor.

You'll have a great time collecting all these oddities like the above: wood, metal and stone are best, if it's plastic, kids USUALLY know its original use!

All manner of interesting 'parts' of old tools, war memorabilia, utensils and supplies will work for your Improv. grab bag.

As an improv warm-up for this more mature group only, have each student go to the front (use mic on a stand if you have one, as it suggests more seriousness to the exercise and we are not working on voice projection in this chapter)! Do NOT give out the props ahead of time to each student, as that gives them a chance to sit there and mull over what they are going to say, thus it is no longer improvisation.

Each student reaches in to a "grab bag" or box, pulls out a prop and is given 30 seconds to turn with back to audience to examine it. You call out "time" after 30 seconds, they turn full front and must 'sell' their prop to the "crowd" like a peddler of new inventions.

They should first tell what it IS, what it's CALLED, what it is used for, how great it is for this purpose, then go into more detail about who invented it, or why and how, where THEY acquired one, perhaps a price, where to acquire one NOW, etc. Give them about 1 to 2 minutes each.

Scene Improvisation Exercise (with Endings given after)

I have at least 30 scenes I've thought up or collected over the years, and I keep these in an index box, with each one printed (print, don't hand-write – it's shocking how few kids can read cursive anymore!) separately on an index card. I have these divided into two groups "Serious" and "Comedic." In many cases, I've also divided these where possible (for a very large class): such as "Two Males, One Female," "Four Females," etc. if you think any of them should be gender specific (see photos).

Above is the box of recipe and index cards I've collected throughout the years, adding new scenes and endings whenever I find one that seems excellent or challenging. Divide your box for Monologues for Girls, Monologues for Boys, Dialogue for Girls, Dialogue for Boys, Dialogue for One Girl and One Boy, Scene with Three: 2 girls and a Boy, etc. etc. etc. I also have a section purely for sparking imaginations in improv, a section just for endings or resolutions, a section for jokes to help with shy ad-libbers at the mic, and cut up cards for an "outta my pocket" exercise which you'll see in a later chapter.

Divide the class into groups, and hand each group one card with a scene. Examples are as follows:

Comedic: a) An astronaut, a pirate and a nurse discuss the nutrition of their "ship-mates." (The pirate is a cannibal, the astronaut is on a liquid diet...)

b) Hansel and Gretel get lost in the woods and meet Harry Potter on his broomstick, who tries to convince them NOT to go inside the cottage.

c) An imposter impersonates a ballet instructor and tries to make her new female students believe in her as she teaches the class

Serious:

a) Two salesclerks, one old, one young, discuss their handsome manager who is middle-aged, each thinking she may have a romantic chance.

b) A doctor, a nurse and a female patient who is recently married, discuss the bruises on her arms and neck, which SHE insists are because she's accident-prone and always bumping in to things.

Give each group three minutes to quickly work out the IDEA (not the actual lines) of their scene which you tell them must be at least three minutes LONG.

■■

You may wish to tell them to make sure they have an obvious ending/resolution of problem, and for everyone to freeze when it's over (so audience knows to clap without some student in the performing group shrugging and saying 'that's it'.

ALTERNATIVELY:

I enjoy giving them the three minutes to quickly work out what they are going to do/say and THEN: I go around and each group draws another index card, at random – these are endings COMPLETELY irrelevant to their scene topic, but somehow they must wrap up the scene to make sense USING THE ENDING THEY'VE DRAWN. This is, of course, quite a challenge!

Examples of endings, which I keep separate in the index box, as they can also be used for other exercises such as CONFLICT RESOLUTIONS, etc. are:

1. A shake of hands—agreement

2. A person goes to sleep

3. A heavy rain causes flooding and everyone must evacuate

4. A song is sung

5. A nearly fatal injury occurs

6. An argument, with a door slamming

••

Give them perhaps another minute or two to work on how the ending will fit in. Stress that it must be somehow relevant to their scene. For example, tell them:

"If you're the pirate and the astronaut and you've drawn the "song to be sung" ending, you should sing something about the food you'll be eating, not TWINKLE, TWINKLE LITTLE STAR.... And if you're the doctor and nurse examining a patient, you can't just suddenly say 'Oh, here comes a flood! Everyone RUN!'"

- *A teachable moment is simply "opportunity knocking" – whenever you have scenery, props or costumes that may lend themselves to improvising a scene – USE THEM! (And never, never listen to your Mom when she says: DON'T make a scene in public!)*

There are many, many more challenging, and just plain fun improvisational exercises in a variety of text books, and also the tv show (still available online) Whose Line is it Anyway? (there are both American and British versions) can give you many ideas. I have tried, here, to use the exercises that I've discovered work best, for certain age groups and abilities.

Chapter 4: Storytelling and Early Characterization Exercises

Introduction to Storytelling and Characters

When there's a story you feel is important

You can tell it, or write it all down

But it will more be remembered

If the princess strides out in her gown,

Or the soldier dies right in front.

Make your story come alive to all

By learning to SHOW how it happens

From the rise to the curtain call.

And children will best learn to study

The characters of all who surround

If each story comes alive from the roles that are played

By the teller who adds sight and sound.

<u>STORYTELLING WITH *CHARACTERS* - DEMO AND INTRO FOR ALL THREE GROUPS</u>

The onus of the first part of this lesson is really on YOU, as the teacher, or workshop leader. You'll have to be prepared ahead of time and choose a story to tell that is suitable for the ages you are working with. I've found, as storyteller, it's best to choose something from your own life, and then just exaggerate the events and the characters to make it more interesting. (Don't we all do this anyway?) That way, you won't forget an important detail, or forget a voice for a certain character. However, if you're confident, then memorize or know VERY well, a story you've chosen – as long as it's age appropriate. (The Group Threes are NOT going to want to hear you re-tell Cinderella, for example).

Explain to your students that you are going to tell a short story, putting a lot of emotion and characterization in to the telling of it. If you like, go into the history of story-telling a bit: i.e.: the caveman's pictographs, the native's fireside legends, also, fables, morals, etc. Or just get on with the story! Tell them that since stories were never READ, just TOLD – they are more conversational and exciting to hear, and more of a "performance" piece.

Warm-Up

When you're finished your story-telling demonstration, ask each person to think of a very short story to tell about any of the following topics:

- A funny event that happened with their pet/sibling
- The time they got lost
- The last family holiday dinner they had, etc.

Then each person comes up and shares, trying to emulate what you did in your Demo. They need a story, with characters' voices, actions, and perhaps even a moral or obvious ending-sentence.

Another warm-up, and greatly supported by young people's modern use of the LOL Cam, is to have the students, no matter what ages, experiment with facial expressions and hand gestures when a particular emotion is suggested. The more expressive they can be (in front of mirrors if you have access), the more they will respond to their characterization exercises.

- *Young people love making faces in the mirror. If you have access, have them do as many as possible, either on their own, or with you calling out various EMOTES. (For instance, call "Horror," "Anger," "Delight.")*
- *Do insist that the children are not playing off each other, but only looking at themselves and concentrating on their OWN faces. This helps, not only with the concentration they will need for*

later exercises, but also assists those who may be self-conscious, to feel less so.

- *If a LOL CAM, or just a regular digital camera is available, ask the students to do 3 to 5 poses each with you calling out the EMOTE, and show them on the camera. You can also have them do several, then show it to another student and ask them to IDENTIFY.*

Character Exercises:

Group One:

The above is probably enough for the younger set. Characterizing is the most difficult and challenging for anyone under age 12 or so. However, if you have time and the props collected to do so, we know kids LOVE to play dress-up, so give each one ONE or TWO special costume-props (see photos) and ask them to become, by walking and talking and miming a particular duty or action, THE CHARACTER THAT THESE SUGGEST. Examples are as follows:

A White Cap and a Pipe– sea captain

Glasses/Specs – old lady; add books: teacher or librarian

Beads and Feathers – a dancer (flapper), a native

Magnifying Glass – a detective

Tall Cane – a shepherd

Big Hook – a pirate

Aged Cream-colored Apron- pioneer lady

Handkerchief (and hat) – cowboy

Fan – southern belle, or Japanese geisha

Closed, dark umbrella with briefcase – business man or woman

Open, light-colored umbrella- Victorian lady, southern belle, etc.

    If you can't get a collection of these items around your house or that of your friends', start collecting just after Halloween when the stores are full of these props (although fake plastic ones) or go to your thrift stores and dig up whatever you can find for inexpensive prices there.

- *The introduction of the simplest hand prop like this magnifying glass can produce dramatic results with even Group One. This young man began to seriously believe he was a great detective!*
- *A simple pair of glasses, whether regular glass, no glass, or tinted can change the very essence of a Group One age's concept of their character. (Then see the variation in glasses or specs that can occur by Group Three, below.)*
- *Throw a handkerchief around a neck and an old beaten-up cowboy hat on, and anyone in Group One knows instantly what they've become!*

- *While the introduction of hand props causes a great stir of excitement in Groups One and Two, it is with Group Three ages that you can allow more subtle variances of these props to make even more eccentric characters come alive (not to mention that umbrellas, shepherd's crooks and pirate's hooks will sometimes prove dangerous with the younger groups!)*
- *From a regular pair of glasses to a regular umbrella, used with Group One, we have altered the props as an exercise in characterization for a Group Three; the glasses have a piece of tape in the middle, the umbrella had lace glued around it. Thus, two completely different characters emerge: a "geek" and a "southern belle" with her parasol.*

Character Exercise, Group Two: "Outta My Pocket"

In preparation for this exercise, have:

copies of SIMPLE scenes or excerpts from CHILDREN's PLAYS,

cut-up recipe or index cards (if recipe cards, cut in thirds, if index cards, cut into eighths). On each card write non-sequitur lines to be spoken like:

- What kind of sick joke are you trying to pull?
- You have a nose like Rudolph.
- I wear pink underwear, you know.
- It's cold in here, where's my ear muffs?

- Don't you DARE kick my dog.
- I wonder about sweat.
- I've eaten a whole chicken.
- Why are you looking at me that way?
- When are we leaving for the bank, anyway?

Etc.

This character development exercise should be given with a short written scene, for two or three people, perhaps four at most. Make this an excerpt chosen from any SIMPLE play that you have, or which can be downloaded from the internet. Scenes are very short – one to two pages in length.

Have each person in each group be a number, eg. 1, 2, 3 and 4. Thus, if you have three groups in the room, you should have three number 1's, and three number 2's. Have each person have a copy of their group's script. Also, give three or four cards to each person, but they are not to look at them and must put them into their pocket, or tuck them into their waistbands. Groups spread out around the room.

Have your groups begin speaking their lines to each other from their copies of run-off scripts, with NO idea what their character might be. Each group can have a different scene, or all could be working on the same scene, as long as they are in different corners of the room.

When you clap your hands they must stop talking/reading immediately and listen to you. Do this about thirty seconds after they've started and call out:

"All number 2's are old people!"

Their scenes continue with the number twos hopefully walking and talking like senior citizens.

Next, clap your hands and call out:

"All number 1's are aliens from outer space (or whatever you like)!"

Next, clap your hands and holler:

"All number 3's are drunk (or whatever you like)!"

Then begin with their pockets. Clap and call out:

"All number 1's, pick a card from your pocket (or waist band) and read what's on it, IN CHARACTER (old, drunk, alien, whatever), at the end of your next scripted line. Everyone in the group should react to that line as their character would, and then proceed with the script!"

Do these pocket lines several more times so everyone gets a few chances. If they come to the end of their scripts, simply have them start again. This is character building at its best, and simplest.

Note: This exercise can also be used for Group Three ages and the Pocket Lines can also be implemented as an additional Improv exercise.

Group Three

Warm-Up

If you have a collection of hats (once again, thrift stores or just after Halloween are best for inexpensive buying!) this is a GREAT warm-up that really only a very mature, thoughtful group can pull off successfully. Sitting in theater circle, have each student try on a hat, and have them pose, frozen-faced, with the expression they think BEST suits the character who would wear that hat (e.g. baseball cap or dilapidated straw hat– face-twisted red-neck chewing something, big feathered lady's hat – a snooty expression, etc.). But then, and this is the most difficult, they should trade hats with others, and you go around the circle while each pose, frozen-faced, with the EXACT OPPOSITE look to the one we would expect with someone wearing that hat (see photos below).

- *The advanced stage: the court jester is in a rage, the police officer is terrified.*
- *As a characterization exercise with Group Threes, hats and even lampshades (on left) can be introduced, with a limitless variety of creative ideas.*
- *The next step is to ask each person, with each hat they try on, to show with gesture or a few words, three to five different characters that might be found wearing their particular style of hat.*

Character Exercise: Photograph or Painting of "Who I Am"

note: Exercise "At My Party" can also be used for Characterization exercise – see it under Improv Chapter.

Collect from magazines, old coffee table books, or the internet, many photographs of intriguing faces, and/or scenes with three or four characters appearing to be doing something interesting. In a pinch I have used Norman Rockwell paintings, but sometimes these are so obviously characterful already that the student doesn't have to do much "work" (thinking) on their own. Have each teen write a paragraph about what their designated character is like, and what they are doing at the moment the photo is taken. Collect these sheets and scan them, making any suggestions, or asking more thought-provoking questions of them. Then each teen goes to the front and tells IN CHARACTER, IN FIRST PERSON, the audience of their PAST HISTORY (not what they just wrote on their pages!). In other words, psychologically why they are the way they are. After this preamble, the audience are allowed to ask questions of them, which they must then answer in character.

The last part of this exercise is to put the class in groups of three to five students. Each person must act IN CHARACTER throughout a short scene that they can

a) improvise from scratch

b) improvise from cards you give them with scene ideas (eg. below)

c) improvise from the photographs (if you gave them scene photos)

OR

d) read from a short scene already prepared (copy from play books, scenes from drama texts, or download from the internet).

Examples of Scenes for Cards

    A taxi driver who is hard of hearing takes a father and son, strangers in a big city and with little money, to the YWCA instead of the YMCA and drives away before they realize.

    Two women in a war-torn country fight over whether the tiny infant skeleton found is their own missing child. A warden comes along to try and mediate.

    Four people are at a small valley-town community meeting and are constantly bickering over whether the town should be bought off by the government to flood for a dam. Though they are offered a great deal of money for their homes, many do not wish to see this happen. A fifth person could be the chairman.

A dog in a park has bitten a small child. The dog was on his leash, and the child had run up and hugged the dog. The owner, the child's mother and a witness are arguing over whether the dog pound should be called to put the dog to sleep.

_____
_____

Note: much has already been stated about accents at the bottom of the chapter on Voice. Please read if there is some question as to whether or not an accent should be promoted.

TIPS FOR THE TEACHER:

Some suggestions if a person is having trouble with characterization: add wigs to your collection, give them two or three hand props instead of one, add a mole or false teeth (see photo) and advise them that being able to :pick one's nose or ear, cry on demand, giggle nervously, raise ONE eyebrow or wink are all extras that can help any character become more distinctive (see photos of girls desperately trying to teach themselves to "raise one eyebrow" when I informed them that this was a highly-sought after skill at any audition!).

Chapter 5: Puppetry Exercises and Tips

Introduction to Puppetry

A puppet is more than a mere child's toy

Much more than a plaything that waves

A puppet can speak when a person can not;

It can reach out! It captures, enslaves

One's heart. Makes all it says

Seem true and so the magic will coax

Strong belief and fantasy

We should all put HOPE in the wee folks!

Warm-Up for All Three Groups

     A warm-up isn't particularly necessary for this, but if you need one just before they actually start to work with the puppets, the age-old partner trick is amusing. (One person is the "front" man or "puppet" and their arms are clasped behind their back. The other person hides behind their back, but puts their arms around them and it is the "back" person whose hands the audience sees. Have them do something simple, like speak or sing while pretending to wash the dishes, or bathe the dog, or eat a meal...)

Group One: That's My Sock!

Everyone knows the easiest way to make a puppet is to use a sock and apply craft-items to make particular faces, expressions, etc. The best exercise for the youngest group is in MAKING their puppet, so have them come prepared with their own wool or part wool sock, if possible, or a long white sweat sock.

Bring items like buttons, yarn, glue, fabric or permanent markers and scissors as some may want to cut holes for a nose or tongue (finger goes through), or to cut two at the side for thumb and little finger to become "arms." If you have a budget to spend, you can buy additional craft items like marbles, pipe cleaners (make accordion-like for bouncy eyes, arms, etc...) doll's eyes, sprinkles, hair, etc.

**Scrim: Cheesecloth
Theatre: Room Divider
(also useful with side room as the back ...)
Puppet: Sock Snake
Sock: Grey Adidas**

Even a sock puppet with no embellishments (upper left) can still have character, but then – put on two puppets and a string of pearls, and VOILA! Miss Marple solves another crime...Above (bottom) is my room divider puppet theater, with Addie, the Adidas Adder, peeking through. The scrim used is cheesecloth-like draperies, but you may want to experiment with heavy black or maroon, depending on the required effect.

Give the children about a half-hour or so to make their puppets. If they finish early, have them practice their puppet's "voice" and have them be prepared to answer questions about their puppet's character.

Put them in groups and have them either a) re-tell, without changing who their puppets' characters are, a well-known fairy tale

Or

b) improvise a short play with a resolution at the end, and even better, a moral to the story.

- *Try to let the children's puppets decide what story they will act out... It is the FACES of their puppets (decided AFTER they have made them and studied them, ideally) that should suggest certain characteristics, and thus stories...*

If you're very enthusiastic and a hobbyist – or live with one – a puppet stage may be built from light wood or plastic. However, they are easy to make from a large cardboard box – ask at your local appliance store for fridge or stove boxes, or check local dumpsters. Simply cut a tv-sized square from one side, and staple a piece of cheesecloth or a thin piece of cotton to the INSIDE of the box, surrounding the hole. Alternatively, I have a room divider (see photo) with curtains pinned to the back and enough "holes" for various puppets to "peek" through as they enter and speak. You may also find something like this serves the purpose.

Group Two - Animal Puppetry

When I was teaching and doing a lot of workshops as well, I found it best to buy and take along a considerable number of animal puppets (when I taught in England I was especially pleased to introduce the children there to animals of which they were not familiar: a raccoon, a beaver, a moose and a grizzly bear, etc.) This of course costs money to collect these, but you can often have great luck doing a circuit of thrift stores and looking in the toy sections. (Wash them before you take them to your class!) Also, just after Christmas, there are a number of sales in educational stores and toy stores on these items, esp. if the puppets are not particularly highly advanced types (ie: nothing more than their two front "paws" move).

- *In the absence of a puppet theater, puppet shows can also be done with blackened stage, and puppeteers in black, with either black nylon pantyhose over their heads, or enhancing their heads only to relate to their puppet.*

In a pinch, collect a lot of very old teddy bears (like in the photo below). These are already thinned out and well-worn/malleable and thus can be easily unstuffed (leave a little in the head). Cut off their legs so that most of the stuffing is removed and presto – an animal puppet! Dress up if you like, or mark with Magic Marker, put on attachments, etc. (ie: a raccoon, bear or deer with stick-antlers can all be made from an old teddy!)

If you can't afford to buy animal puppets, collect anyone's old teddy bears – those who are willing to part with them (and not witness the surgery you're about to perform!) Cut off the bears about half way down their bellies, pull most of the stuffing out, leaving a little in the head only. Make sure thumbs and pinkies will fit in the teddy bears' arms, and then decorate to make the required animal!

If you have time beforehand, ask each child to bring in one puppet (they shouldn't be allowed to be the voice/character of the puppet they bring in, however; it's more of a stretch for them to work with the unfamiliar!). This at least gives you just enough puppets to give some variety.

Put the children in groups. Have children's stories with animals as the key roles. Give each group a storybook, which one of the children reads aloud to their group. It doesn't matter if the animals in the story are the same as the ones they will be puppeteering; they will have to be flexible enough to change the names, etc.

They are then to improvise a puppet play using the basic ideas from the story book, or at the very least, have their parents bring in their younger siblings to watch at the end of the lesson.

One of my professional theater "roles" was as Mother Nature in a provincial park each summer season, performing with animal puppets whose "voices"

explained to children about their habitat, their eating habits, their winter survival and their predators. Education is often best relayed to the young in an entertaining format.

Group Three – Marionettes or Cut-Outs

If you can manage to collect about three marionettes (or more) from your friends/family OR from the students themselves beforehand, you don't need too many for this section/age group.

If you can NOT find marionettes, have them make the cut-outs with plenty of cardboard, bristol board, magazines and craft supplies (see photos).

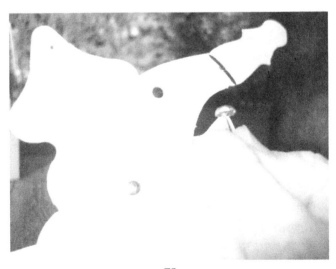

First, cut out full-length people from old text books, paper doll books, magazines, or enlarge on photocopiers any such items from the internet. Then, cut out on bristol board or white card, the same shape. Glue to the back of your cut-out. Then cut off the arms and legs at all the joints (or as many as you prefer) make small holes with a large embroidery needle, and re-apply the limbs at the joints with a fold-back pin (shown). The arm-pits and pelvis of both sides should be attached to the main popsicle stick, doctor's stick or piece of cardboard for the main 'handle', but should not go all the way through to the front (below).

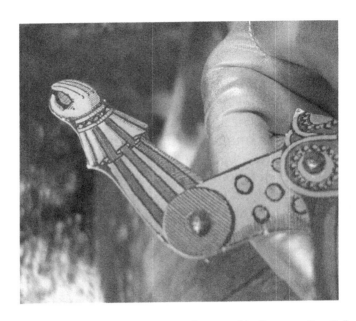

A drinking straw may then be applied to each of the forearms, and lower legs, especially if there will be additional puppeteers on each.

Ideally, puppeteers should wear long black gloves if presenting in a puppet theater, but in this case, the demonstrator wears gloves more likely to fit in to the outdoor background and table. If the puppeteer sticks their hands through a white sheet or curtain, they should wear long WHITE gloves.

This particular "jumping jack" court jester cut-out came from a "kit," but they are equally as easy and fun to make from scratch...

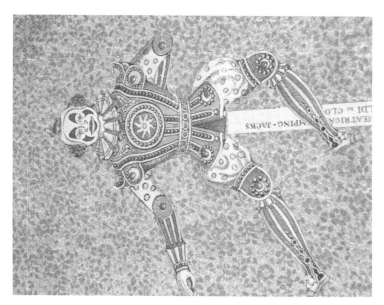

A cut-out with extra wires or drinking straws on other parts of the limbs can be handled by different puppeteers so that the character moves more fluidly and more life-like.

I also begin this section by showing the Goatherd Puppet Show from The Sound of Music.

If you're using marionettes, a fridge box or a U-Haul box for a stand-up closet works well, so that the teens can stand up in it. Have arm-holes cut out, and make a small platform about a foot or so off the ground on the audience side. (My room divider also works for marionette plays- see photo.)

If you're using cut-outs, the standard puppet show stage is best.
■ ■

For a marionette exercise, put in groups of however many marionettes you have at your disposal. Do NOT let any group have the puppets yet, however. They have seen them, and know what kind of character they might like to develop around the puppets, but that is all at this time.

Each group must then make up, together, a short play about five minutes long. (If you wish, and you know what the puppets will look like ahead of time, you can have suggestions for scenes on cards for them to draw). Rather than improvising a puppet show, which does NOT work well, this should be a fully-rehearsed production, so have them go over and over their lines. As you are making your tours of the room, you'll see which group is best prepared, and they may work with the box/stage and the marionettes first. This, then, spurs the other groups on to get their lines down.

After each group has had a rehearsal time with the stage and puppets, you may, if time isn't a factor, ask them to perform for the rest of the group (or their parents if they are being picked up near the end of the lesson).

Like Group Two, one or more of these groups may want to present outside of their environs, and if time is not a constraint and parents are willing, I suggest this age group go to senior's homes to entertain.
■■

For a cut-out show, the crafting will take up most of one lesson, and you want them to look as professional as possible. As cut-outs are small, I often suggest that teens (being what they are technologically today) video and share these puppet shows on Facebook or YouTube. Having this goal as a finished production gives them more interest in making their cut-outs look and sound professional.

Again, put them in groups, let them rehearse their lines without the movements of their puppets, and then let one group at a time rehearse in the stage area.

Then, set up a performance time, with the lights dark, some light (overhead projector, flashlight, whatever) on the stage, and several teens taking the video – one with close-ups, one with overall long shots. If they are really good, one or two may even offer to edit these together before making the videos "public."

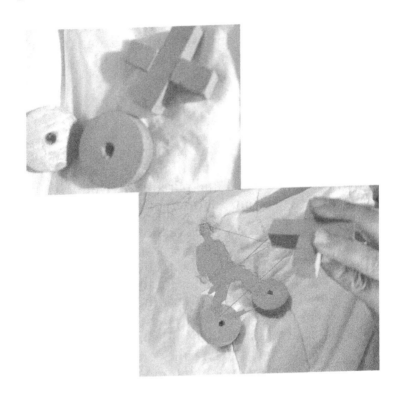

If you have the time and desire, you can make yourself a collection of marionettes by starting simply with a wooden cross (popsicle sticks work, too) and a couple of wooden circles for feet-weights (can use large wooden beads or wooden car wheels, bought separately in craft shops). Then make yourself a raggedy-type doll, or mini-scarecrow (raffia works well for this), dress it up and attach your strings or fishing line.

Chapter 6: Early Stage Conflict and Fight Scenes

Introduction to Dramatic Physical Conflicts

Children love to wrestle,

Or pull a sword out and go "stab"

But the essence of this chapter is

To teach more GIVE than GRAB.

Stage fighting is about the dance,

The generosity of space

It's not about the win or lose,

It's about who can give their place.

So someone ELSE appears to "win."

To teach this to the young

Will make you old before your time!

- *YOU'LL be that hero YET UNSUNG!*

This MAY not be a section of your planning that you wish to even attempt. No matter what your experience, if you have more than 6 children or younger teens, I HIGHLY suggest you have some parental volunteers or teaching assistants in the room because your eyes simply can not be everywhere, and no matter what type of props you choose to use, it will get everyone VERY excited!

Warm-Up for All Groups

Have a Choreograph pre-planned before you begin and this is one time when pairs are actually preferred. (You may have to ask one of your volunteers to be odd man out). I still recommend you put them in pairs yourself, to avoid hurt feelings – jus' say, like the Dance Sticks in the Movement section- that they should be a similar height.

Teach one movement at a time. For example –

Two arms cross each other – call it "cross."

One partner steps in with a head butt – call it "head."

Both partners step away from each other – call it "back."

One takes another's arm and pulls them down – call it "down."

Then gradually add them in, one at a time until the whole "dance" is choreographed, with you calling each out, and counting a 1,2,3, hold until the next step.

Group One and Group Two

The Magic Wand

This is an inexpensive way for you to teach some of the physical conflicts necessary. Collect wrapping paper cardboard inserts, or better yet, a roll from vinyl, or plastic table cloth in rolls. The latter are heavier and longer, which is preferable.

Both Groups One and Two can use this exercise quite satisfactorily.

Start with a group of three or four, each student taking a turn to handle the "wand" on their own. Have them practice twirling it, (simulates martial arts), hopping over it, stabbing it into the air, leaning on it, etc.

- *The Magic Cardboard Wand - The simple, inexpensive and most important of all – SAFE! - fighting weapon!*

Then practice with them "attacking" another in the same types of ways – they "stab" or run and "joust," while the others duck, somersault (if you're lucky enough to have mats at your disposal), and hop over the "wand" as it is swung toward them. Have the group work on 6 or 7 positions together, and each person with the wand in hand (it may of course be grabbed away IF PLANNED) must yell their numbers out in "anger." So, for example – swing "one, one, ONE!," step over and glare 'two, two, TWO!," etc. (see photographs).

- *The next stage of this use of the Magic Wand in groups is to have each group choreograph their own short fight scene. They may add a few lines, or vocal noises, shouts, grunts, etc. if they wish.*

Group Three

Slaps, Punches, and Push/Pulls

Assuming that, as a warm-up, the pre-planned choreograph has been also done with this group, the more mature might move on to the following as a more VOCAL conflict (which MIGHT introduce some improvisational physical conflict toward the end.)

Groups of three work best for this exercise, "I Want the Chair." Have one person sit on a chair or stool. Two others come along and for whatever reasons (improvised as they discuss) one of the two DESPERATELY needs to sit on this chair. The first person does not think it is a good-enough reason and will staunchly refuse, for reasons of their own (improvised) which they continually vocalize. As with any conflict, a resolution of some sort is needed, so be sure your instructions are only that after several minutes, the problem "must be solved," but of course it does not have to be a satisfactory solution to ALL involved!

I once had a group improvise the following scenario:

Instead of the usual and predictable " my mother is disabled" or "I really, really have to go to the bathroom" reasons for needing to sit, the two who entered insisted, without at first explaining why (the Hidden Agenda, perfect for this exercise if you wish to set them all up with one..) that they HAD to "examine" the chair. This was truly inventive, and as I watched, they fought with the seated person until she was prone on the floor "knocked out, "then proceeded to "rip apart" the chair in their search for the treasure their Pirate King had hidden there 5 years ago.

This was SO inventive and creative, thought up within the confines of improv., that I allowed them to perform it to the class. However, do please note that time constraints don't usually allow for EVERYONE to "present" ANY of these exercises in this book, and there are other reasons for not doing so: a) many young people WANT to perform and are giddy with the "high" of over-acting in front of their peers. It is often better for them to learn to simply "share" the work, and that it is the Quality of this work for which

YOU as teacher are looking, not how well they outshine "on-stage."

b) Alternatively, of course, there are the many children who have been enrolled by their parents to try and rid them of shyness, and it doesn't help the cause if they are continually asked to "perform." They will get enough just interacting with these excellent exercises, and perhaps the odd presentation here or there, depending on the time of the lesson(s).

Thus, it is best for all of Drama Workshopping, if you as leader, and your adult assistants, simply tour the room, watching, perhaps giving a small direction or correction here and there if need be, and then praising the work.

Now, for the physical conflicts for Group Three.

TEACHING A STAGE SLAP

There are many opinions on how this should be taught to teenagers. Some stage slaps are SO fake-looking, you wish they'd never been used. But it is, perhaps, a good idea to teach all possibilities and let the groups decide for themselves what they feel works best.

- One method is for the slapper to cup their hand so the sting is minimized, and the noise amplified (often in addition to a sound effect, either the slappee hitting their upstage –away from audience, see glossary of terms – leg,

themselves, or by an offstage 'slap' sound.) The slapping hand should ALWAYS be at least two inches down from the ear, and NEVER hit the neck!
- Another method is not to touch the cheek at all, but for the slapper to "hit" (simulated) with their upstage hand while one of the above sounds are affected.
- The best, and certainly most mature method, is for a "real" slap to be emitted. Not with the force of a major swing, obviously, but when using the upstage hand and cheek, the audience doesn't see as much anyway. The important thing is for the slapper NOT to slow down their hand an inch away from the slappee's cheek, and this, I maintain, is always the problem in those very fake slaps we've all seen. Follow through, and then the slappee should instantly upon contact move their head downstage away from the slap, rendering two things a) less force and b) a bigger "production" for the audience to see, ie: startled eyes, raised eyebrows, shock, hurt, etc.

I would advise the groups attempt all variations on the stage slap, and each person in the group should have a chance at being both the slapper and the slappee.

The Stage Punch

The only punches we teach to teens are the "gut" punch and the "upper" to the jaw. Both are difficult to teach, but obviously the gut is simpler. As with the slap it is important that the fist of the thrower be loose, not tightly clasped, and that the follow-through not stop an inch away from its target. The receiver should instantly double over as the fist is about an inch away, however, and loose clothing on the costume can help this immensely. Also, it is better that, rather than being parallel to the audience which is best for the slap, the receiver be downstage slightly, with their back ¾ turned to the audience, and the thrower be upstage, primarily FACING the audience.

The same should be said of the upper, but this is much trickier to affect when allowing teens to do this and it should be practiced many, many times in slow motion first, and possibly NEVER (depending on the maturity and ability of the groups) allowed to be put into normal-speed action!

Push/Pulls

These can be anywhere from mild to appearing quite violent, culminating in all types of falls and crashes through props, depending on what mats and stage devices you have at your disposal. It is really the After-effect (the fall/crash) that is most impressive to the audience. (I once had the great delight of pushing a fellow cast member twice my size, into a 'glass' coffee table and watching night after night as the 'fake' sugar-glass crystallized around him with no end of tinklings as well as shocked gasps from the audience. Most satisfactory and therapeutic, but very few companies can afford endless sheets of stage 'coffee table' tops, windows or etc.)

It's best if the violator grasps the clothing of his victim, rather than their actual bones and skin. Obviously, if you're grabbing the arm of a Victorian damsel in tight lace sleeves, or grasping from the floor the leg of a Medieval courtier in leggings, this is impossible, but with careful, premeditated costuming, direction and choreography, no bruises should emanate.

A hefty push in the back is most effective, and as it's expected, the pushed can make the most of a dramatic stumble or tumble immediately following. Pulling, with an extra swing about-face, is also very effective, especially if the clothing rips (most Dames of Wardrobe will beg the director not to choreograph this way, but it DOES make for audience titillation!).

I do not EVER recommend allowing any young people to practice any type of kicks, or martial art movements, or even "shootings," though some wise one will invariably request to do so (or worse yet, "improvise" such a maneuver).

As a final note to this section, if you can get any expert in (a choreographer, martial arts expert or stunt person) to speak with your students and perhaps give some demonstrations, half the battle for you is won. The students, no matter what their ages, will be thrilled and you will not actually have to have them enact so many gestures themselves. I once had a close friend who had been a stunt man for Burt Reynolds (the one who slides under the truck at the beginning of Smokey and the Bandit). He came to speak to a drama workshop I'd set up, and both children and adults listened spell-bound, and watched on video his every move, in slow motion to enhance the disciplined choreography behind it. They left with a new respect for rehearsing again and again something that should appear impulsive and forceful, but which is in fact nothing more than a dance.

TIPS FOR THE TEACHER:

There are many text books written on Stage Techniques, where you will find more ideas for teaching fight scenes, shooting scenes, and death scenes. Judge your Group Three on their maturity and decide for yourself what you think they can handle in teaching conflicts. One note: DO teach that when anyone falls, they should ALWAYS do it in stages or degrees (whether or not there is a mat on the floor for them!) Ideally, the weight should be placed on the leg opposite from the side on which the student will fall. And NEVER (unless a slapstick comedy) allow the feet to flip up after the fall is complete!

If you have a truly remarkable and mature Group Three, then by all means introduce sword fighting, even if they are just the plastic things you buy after Halloween, on sale. Choreograph various routines with the swords, and if possible, have a fencing instructor come in as a guest and to demonstrate (your students MAY even be allowed to handle the real swords in this case!). Tip: If you do introduce sword fighting, or for any of the conflicts taught, you MAY want to show a clip from the movie the Princess Bride – fairly near the beginning, when there is the magnificently choreographed sword scene on top of the high cliffs.

Chapter 7: Clowning and Mask Exercises and Tips

Introduction to Clowning and Masks

Our faces show so much emotion

If covered, what can we convey?

If a bag's o'er our head or a mask on our face

Can we still act our part in the play?

We must use the tools that change who we are

Like a clown nose gives freedom because

It allows us to instantly be someone else

And we now do what THAT "someone" does!

      This component of Drama may seem to some to be an ironic dichotomy of the clichéd connotation of "clowning." I would even venture to say that this chapter is perhaps to be taken the MOST seriously of any, and that it may also need to ONLY be done with

Group Threes, depending on the maturity of other ages with which you'll be working.

Sometimes, "Mime" is taught under this category; sometimes it is taught under Movement. I am not going to present any exercises at all for this as I believe mime is best left until college level.

If you DO decide to do some mask or nose work with younger groups, don't TELL them about the noses and masks ahead of time. I suggest first "testing" them by saying, just as an "exercise" you want them to do, that they must make a mask with their fingers, then do facial studies as illustrated below in the photographs. If they can not do these seriously, you should not continue with the exercises laid out for Group Threes. Don't treat this as a punishment, but just see how the finger-mask facial studies work out.

- *Have the younger children work on a "finger mask" to attempt facial study. If you want to make it more "exciting" for them, they can put on gloves. Black or navy blue work best, as they enhance the eyes and mouth.*
- *As described in the Group Three exercise below, have the young people study the faces, and changes to the faces their 'masks' make. What are the eyes like? Are the mouths partially hidden? What do their partners' teeth look like? Etc. Etc.*
- *If the children cannot perform this simple exercise without laughing or giggling or looking elsewhere other than their partner's eyes for a facial study of at least 2 minutes, then do not*

continue with half-masks or clown noses as outlined for Group Three.

- *If, however, you have a group of younger children who CAN manage the finger-mask facial studies for periods of 2 minutes or more (try with several different partners, as well), then by all means, try the clown noses and half-masks as set out for the Group Threes. It will be rare, however, that you will have a group of under-teens who can concentrate seriously on this. In fact, you will often have to chastise even the Group Three levels re: their attention and concentration.*

Group Three:

    Making papier mache masks to perfectly fit the face of each student is not something I personally have done with any drama lessons for young people – I have always invited experts in to teach this section if I wish it to be a component. It can be scary to many to MAKE the masks (quite an involved process if done properly), just as seeing others wearing masks or clown noses can be truly TERRIFYING to others. (When I was clowning professionally, I often had children run out of the room to their mothers, but if I just went to them and showed them my taking off of the nose and spoke to them in my normal voice (TWO "NO-NO'S", by the way, when you're TEACHING the art of clowning) they would relax.   If this is to be a long lesson (ie: a whole unit in a school year), invest (again, after Halloween is best) in some plastic masks. I have tried to buy enough that everyone wears the same at first, so we don't have anyone upstaging or performing additional and unwanted "antics." I also try, USUALLY, to purchase plain-colored, unembellished ones (like the black, far right, in below photos). Half-face is better to start with than full-face, as any lines they speak will not be muffled (see photos).

- *It is recommended that students have several moments in front of a mirror, on their own with no interactions, to decide on the "character" or "emotion" that their new face represents or symbolizes.*
- *If you make your full-face mask from a paper bag, make sure you do give the eyes some highlight to enhance the same shape as the cut-outs. White full-face masks such as the one above, work BEAUTIFULLY to complement a clown nose, rather than doing grease-painting of face.*
- *Once a "full-face" has been created (either by an actual full-face mask, or by a paper-bag or grease-painted face, the half mask can also then be used to add variations to age, symbolic theme, sex, emotion, etc.*

If you're really not prepared to spend any money, or can't find masks, a brown paper bag for each student with the eyes and mouth cut out work just fine.

I have also finally invested in good sponge clown noses, the type that will stay on without slipping.

The above are the best kind of clown noses, if you can afford to invest in them. There are, however, many other inexpensive ways for having students "feel" the same effect!

The sponge noses have a slit, with extra ventilation for the nostrils, and as they are sponge, are therefore non-slip. Note also in this photo, the long glove suggested later in this chapter, for use with masks. Age and Race are thus never an obvious "give-away."

However, a bit of plasticine will help the plastic noses stay on, and if you can't afford or find THEM, buy some light little plastic balls (red isn't necessary, but is usual) and put a slit on one side – not TOO big! If you're REALLY on a budget or have shopping-time constraints, gather up some stick-on bows from last Christmas. It's the IDEA of changing one's face and having an extra appendage which will automatically change one's character that you are trying to teach here, not how they LOOK in their noses or masks.

- *Another tip for an inexpensive clown nose – rummage through your Christmas decor and find all the red or pink sticky-backed bows you can find. They work every bit as well for the identity "feel."*

EXERCISE #1: THE STUDY

Though pairs are not my favourite group, they again work best for this first exercise as with three someone will feel less intently examined.

Each pair studies their partner without saying a word, seriously taking in not just the nose or mask, but their partner's eyes, lips, ears. Each child should present the character that the mask or nose suggests

WITHOUT speaking, at first. When you call out "Time," give them a full five minutes at least for this initial examination, they then add sounds only, such as grunts, humming, clearing the throat or chuckling. These non-verbals will help establish their character even more.

Next, they may add a hand gesture to help add to the character, and lastly, when you once more call "time," they can converse IN THE CHARACTER that has been suggested to them internally by their EXTERNAL appendage. (This is why it is so important to have matching noses or masks for all, at first.)

The pairs may then switch, and the same process is run again.

Then change to either masks or noses, whichever wasn't done in the first instance, and have them trade partners again and repeat the whole process once or twice more.

EXERCISE #2: (TO TAKE PLACE ONLY AFTER EXERCISE #1 HAS BEEN COMPLETED SATISFACTORILY IN SEVERAL DIFFERENT SETS/PAIRS.)

Sometimes, in Asian theater especially, colour and symbolism are an important dynamic of Clowning and Masks. It is often the particular color or shape of a mask that suggests to the audience a recognizable character or figure in myth/history. Long gloves, too, of various colours are often worn to hide, for instance, skin color or wrinkles or the absence of. The purpose of full face masks and/or clown face, is that NO ONE should ever know anything about the REAL identity of the person behind.

Not age, not race, not idiosyncrasies in gesture, etc.

When exercise 1, above, has been completed to satisfaction, take the time to discuss with your students what their concept of masks, face-painting, or clowning is. For the most part, you will hear about humor, balloon animals or balloon hats, and Halloween spooks or Spiderman.

It is important to emphasize that once a full mask or clown nose and painted face has been applied, it NEVER changes. Thus, the character remains consistent in voice, movement, gestures, etc. Explain that being a party clown, or a circus clown is very different from the original COURT JESTER, who would often use metaphor and riddle to show ironic morals in life, not to just "make the king and audience have a giggle."

Also, discuss how a full mask can enhance anonymity and represent such common themes as a: tragedy, comedy, aging, evil, angelic intervention, etc. The mere appearance of these masks on people onstage can change the audience's understanding of where the thread of the plot is going. And of course, they can also be used to disguise a character who must appear more than once, as two or more different roles.

After you have completed this discussion with the students, pass out the masks (or, if using paper bags, I suggest you have different shapes for the cut-outs of eyes and mouth, some slanting up, some down, some wide-eyed and innocent, etc.).

If you choose to do clown-make-up as full face, (then add the nose), have the students choose what they wish from the following:

- Grieving
- Excited
- Worried
- Grumpy
- Silly
- Obnoxious

And etc. There should be at least several DIFFERENT types in the room to continue with the exercise.

Next, you and your assistants apply the greasepaint. This will take an extra session to accomplish this, as well as volunteers, the expense of the makeup, and the patience of the group. I do NOT recommend letting the teens go at the makeup themselves; a great deal will be wasted, the cold cream base will be forgotten, and chances are you won't get the required look on each respective face.

Now, with either the full-masks (commercial or grocery-bagged), or the full-face clowns, allow each student to have two minutes in front of some mirrors so they can judge for themselves what they think their character should symbolize. Then, have two rows of the students, facing each other. Ask them to stand or sit the way they think their character is best represented.

Choose from some of the scenario examples from the other chapters (improv or character-building) or use the examples below. Read out two or three, if you have three or four per group. Walk up and down the middle of the two rows as you do so. Point to one person, who must then say what role the person across from them should play, depending on their facial appearance and their stance or position. For example:

You read "Scenario One" – two tourists are standing at Niagara Falls. One gets on the railing to have a better and falls over. A security person, new at the job, comes along and tries to help in the search. Either successfully or unsuccessfully is up to your group.

Tell them that no words will be spoken, but non-verbal sounds are fine (as practiced in Exercise #1). Then say:

Jack, look across at Evan (directly across in the line). What part do you think he should play in that scenario?"

And Jack casts Evan, perhaps, as the nervous security officer, or the worried tourist.

Once all the parts are cast, in whatever scenarios you've put up for offer, have them work on their scenes.

A few other scenario examples good for Masks/Noses:

A person shows up with a dog (not mimed, but also played by a student, with full character), thinking they have the right house for their new dog-sitting service. Through gestures, and non-verbal sounds, it becomes apparent that the person who answered the door is NOT the right person, and that they have arrived at the wrong house.

In the park, a young baby (played by a student) becomes so animated playing in the sand box that an older child gets a mouthful of sand. They each run to get a parent/nanny/minder and try, through gestures, to explain what went on.

Tips: Remind the students that with non-verbal scenes, overexaggerated gestures are acceptable, and in fact recommended. This is one time where being OVERLY dramatic or melodramatic is actually encouraged.

Chapter 8: Choreographed Steps and Simple Chorus Line Work

Introduction to Chorus Line Stepping/Dance

Broadway! West End! We love our musicals!

To see the kicks and fancy steps upon the throbbing stage

Learning the chorus-line dance-steps

Is good discipline at any age.

Link arms, jump right, stop and twirl, then LEAP!

Great exercise, good memory work, and team work too is here

Step by step we practice

For performances throughout the year...

I have been remiss in mentioning stretching exercises for all the physical components of this book, and, though it is of course important in such areas as Movement, Physical Conflict and others, children are more nimble and will not feel the after effects of strenuous exercise as we do. However, this chapter MUST begin with some stretching exercises on the floor. Basic stretches such as toe-touches, leg raises, arm circles, ankle circles, knee bends, etc. are all that is truly needed.

GROUP ONE: MARCHING BAND

Any good drama teacher or leader "worth their weight" should have a box of percussion-type instruments for various marches, especially with this younger group. The instruments should either be small enough to enable other things to be done with their arms and hands, or, in the case of a drum or tambourine, should hang around the child's neck.

Many rooms will not have a piano, and there will rarely be a pianist available for such exercises as Dancing Sticks, 3 Poses, Chorus Line Dancing and Marches. If you play yourself, it is STILL tricky to keep an eye on the children prancing about whilst you bang out some chords and a melody. So, a box of tambourines, drums and snares, bells, whistles, harmonicas, maracas, and etc. is a useful tool. Even if you have to make these, and spray-paint them up a bit so the children think they are "the real thing," an ice cream or frozen yogurt tub makes an excellent drum, a plastic jar with seeds makes a good "shaker," spoons can take the place of the bells on a tambourine, and banging on pots with a stick will beautifully help keep time – and migraines- in the forefront.

It is so important for MANY different Drama Exercise, but especially this one, to have some percussion –type instruments for the Group One students, and if you haven't got them, they are simple to make/collect from your pots and pans!

Teaching timing with this youngest group is the most important part of this musical step-learning. First, play a song (recorded, or on piano) and have them just march to it, while rubbing their bellies and tapping their heads. This will prove tricky enough for many, and you may have to repeat the song a few times. Next, tell them a particular part of the song (like the repeated chorus), is where they will stop, face the "audience" or FRONT OF HOUSE area and march in place. While doing this, you want, for instance, section one to swing their arms up and to the right, while section two swings up and to the left (or however you'd like to divide it). At the end of that section (whether chorus, or end of song) have them link arms and do a twirl with their partner and a little chorus-line kick in the air to finish off.

The last step is for them to march through the whole song, playing out beats and rhythms on their instruments, while still managing the extra steps, swings, etc. they've been taught. All of this will take considerable practice with this group, so be prepared!

GROUPS TWO AND THREE

These two age-groups can manage a proper lesson in choreography. Study the basic steps which you've probably done before, either in old aerobics classes, or western line dancing, or etc. The "grapevine" is probably the most common one. Inventing your own kicks, knees up, arm waves, etc. is perfectly possible as well, of course.

Teach the order of the steps without music. The best way for this to be taught is to have everyone in a line facing you, and you turn your back to them and dance the steps – first having them watch you, then having them emulate.

- *In both teaching the steps, or just organizing the sound and attention levels (depending on the size of your group), you will have to make sure you have a loud voice, and always appear in control and to know exactly what you're doing. The slightest hint of uncertainty on your part, or a misstep, will result in the students' losing their concentration and even their faith in you as their leader.*

Piece the counts (measures) and steps themselves together, practicing each several times before adding the next. When is seems that they have got it, put it to your music. Show tunes from actual Broadway musicals are still my favorites to use – don't use any of the solo songs, but the ones in which the entire cast/chorus is involved. Alternatively, the Boston Pops or the old Hooked on Classics (where a tacky clapping to the beat is ongoing throughout like a metronome) work as well.

TIPS FOR THE TEACHER:

If a student seems particularly ill-at-ease with the thought of dancing of any kind, or is willing to try, but is simply NOT getting the rhythms or remembering any of the steps, take them aside and offer them one of your percussion instruments. They may then take part either DOWNSTAGE CENTER, as if leading the whole group, but in fact only marching and playing in place OR, they may be off to the side "accompanying" his peers. If they feel confident with this, you could just add a spin or a kick in for them at the end.

- *In this day and age, with all the media attention, DANCING of any type, no matter WHAT one's shape or size or weight, should be a true expression of joy and freedom. It always warms my heart to see the intimacy shared between chorus liners – much more so than most team sports!*

Chapter 9: Scene Work and Skits

Introduction to Scene Work

The basics, for actors, is scene work

Learning lines, moving here, just on cue

It's a discipline used to teach much in life

For it may go against what we'd normally do

So it's best that we stretch to a length

That moulds us opposite truth

We learn to be open, more flexible, so –

It's best to teach this in our YOUTH!

EXERCISE #1 FOR ALL GROUPS

Tableaux:

Tableaux can also be taught in conjunction with either Movement, or with Character/Storytelling, but I personally prefer it as an introduction to Scene Work.

Give some scenarios from your own collection or I like to use news articles from around the world. War scenes/stories are especially poignant.

Give a scene or article to each group. I suggest larger groups – perhaps 5-7 in a group. If your group is small, just use the WHOLE class, OR make sure you have a suitable scenario or news article for only 3 people.

Each group has a volunteer read the scene or article aloud. They will then break the story into 3 or 4 "freeze-frames" (done in silence – no narration or exposition of the scene; the freeze of the scene MUST explain itself!). Remind the group that height can say a lot about a person's superiority over another (thus some crouch of lay down while others may stand on a chair or box), and body language such as lying in a fetal position can immediately show despair or low-self-esteem or fear.

When they are ready to present, have them hold each freeze frame (an action shot, but stopped in time like a photograph by a news journalist) for about 8 seconds. If you like, you can clap your hands or call "next" so that they flow into the next scene by moving quickly and fluidly into their next position. If you do so, this should be THE ONLY SOUND HEARD.

(refer back to similarities in "Three Poses" Exercise under Movement)

GROUP ONE: SCENES FOR THE YOUNGER CHILDREN

Either script out yourself in large printed type, the lines for a fairy tale or legend, OR make sure you've found an age-appropriate short script (2-4 pages of lines, with an equal weight of line distribution given to each character).

Divide up into groups based on the number of people in each scene. Have the groups work on their own ideas for blocking, props, etc. which they can tell you about, or even write down. Memory work should be stressed here, but at this younger age, I would allow, at worst, a prompter – and at best, would allow carrying the script or cue cards with them, providing they seem to "know" their parts sufficiently well.

GROUP TWO: SOME SUGGESTED SCENES FOR THE PRE-TEENS

Diary of Anne Frank – especially the scene where the families celebrate Hanukkah

Arsenic and Old Lace – especially the scene where Mortime has just discovered his old aunts have murdered several gentlemen.

"TWELVE!!" (to be exact...)

Blithe Spirit, etc.

You may also introduce dialogue (for two) and monologue (for one) scenes at this juncture, if your group is quite mature.

Group Three: Some Suggested Scenes for Teens

The Importance of Being Earnest – especially when Lady Bracknell confronts Jack

Impromptu – especially the opening scene

Saint Joan

Diary of Anne Frank

A Raisin in the Sun

More serious scenes in this group should be introduced as opposed to Group Two, where the scenes should be lighter.

TIPS FOR THE TEACHER:

There are SO many scenes which can be found in play books, or downloaded from the internet – just make sure they are age appropriate, somewhat politically correct (unless you want to explain why "nigger" WAS once an accepted word in the south, and how "gay" meant happy, etc.) and don't have anything too violent or sexually connotative within them.

I have also purposely strayed away from the teaching of stage kisses and the like. Very awkward to teach at these ages, and while I had a "peck-on-the-cheek" stage kiss in high school, my first passionate on-stage embrace and kiss was not until I was in my late twenties, so college levels should be soon enough for these techniques to be introduced. Thus, don't choose scenes with intimacy in them! (Unless, perhaps a Mom gives a daughter a hug or some such...)

Also, if there are no time constraints, I do recommend teaching dialogue and monologue to this group, but do so AFTER they have tried presenting a short larger-cast scene. There is less memory work, and less to block on stage.

Skits, especially comedic ones, are often more complicated to have performed WELL. Kids will think they can "do whatever" in a skit, throw pies in faces at irrelevant moments, etc. If skit scenes are to be self-written, have them seriously sit down, discuss, brainstorm and write out their lines, not straying far from their originals as they go into rehearsals for the skits. Unlike presenting play scenes, skits can have a beginning and ending, but should ideally be no longer than 10 minutes. I have had many older kids steal Saturday Night Live or SCTV comedic skits to emulate, and these usually work somewhat better than having them write their own.

Glossary of Basic Theater Terms Used in this Text

Ad-Lib – the improvisation of any stage business or conversation, meaning "at liberty."

Apron – the front of the stage, from the curtain out to the edge.

Audition – a tryout for a position in a play.

Backstage – the areas behind the set not visible to the audience, including the wings, dressing rooms, prop rooms, the green room (lounge for actors) workshops, offices and storage areas.

Blocking – The movements of an actor upon the stage, usually as laid out by the director; however, they are sometimes written in as stage directions by the playwright.

Business – Various motions or actions done by an actor, usually directed by the playwright or director, such as "he picks up book and crosses DL." Any stage business should always have a purpose, the actor motivated do perform it because of plot development, character revelation, etc.

Cross – When an actor makes a large move **across** the stage, from point A to point B, with a particular purpose (motivation) for doing so.

Cue – The last action or line, or tech. effect such as a light dimming that gives notice to an actor to do something. In other words, a signal given from the stage.

Downstage – The front third of the stage, closest to the audience. In Shakespearean time, the stages were tilted (or actually 'raked', as they were originally just mounds of earth!) toward the audience (who stood in crowds on level ground below). The other two thirds of the stage are divided as "Center" and "Upstage," the latter being the very back, away from the audience (the part that used to be elevated the highest for the audience's best viewing).

Front of House, or FOH – All areas of a theater NOT concerned with the stage, or back-stage (such as wings, dressing rooms, etc.) to which the general public might have access. Thus, the audience seats, the lobby, the ticket booths and etc.

Full-Front – When an actor is "blocked' by the director to stand facing the audience squarely, as opposed to other positions which I will not go in to here, such as "three-quarter front," "profile right," etc.

Improvisation – The impromptu portrayal of a character or scene without any preparation or rehearsal given for it. "On the Spot," or "Ad-Lib."

Lead – Short for "leading role," the main characters in the play – usually one female and one male lead.

Left (L) and Right (R) – The sections of the stage from the ACTOR'S point of view, not the director/audience. (Thus, as a teacher standing FOH or at the base of the Apron, you will be directing Blocking by saying "Now cross Stage Right," but it is actually your left.)

Line – Words spoken by actors when on stage. Calling "Line" to a prompter, stage manager or director, is usually only done in rehearsals, when a cue is needed to remind the actor of their line. The cue is usually the first four or five words of the line.

Mime – Born from pantomime, which was a symbolic play of abstract or generally known ideas. Mime is now considered to be for the highly skilled only, as no words are spoken to convey meaning, only carefully enhanced movement and gesture and expression.

Motivation – The reason (not always known by anyone but the actor) behind a character's behavior or words. An actor should never feel that they are moving without purpose, thus at least in their own minds, as reason must be established.

Off, OR Offstage – In the wings, or just slightly backstage; just out of visible range from the audience.

Prompter – The person who keeps, during the course of a play's "run," the director's script, making notes on cues, signals, etc, and who will call out lines if an actor's memorization is lacking.

Props – Short for "properties," but now almost always referred to simply as props. These can be larger items such as a lamp, or smaller such as coins in a pocket, but are anything carried on or off by an actor during the course of the play.

Scenario – The premise behind a scene, the main idea that should be conveyed, the plot outline.

Scrim – A backdrop cloth made of fabric that is opaque when lit from the front, and semi-transparent when lit from behind (good for foggy scenes or dream sequences, or some type of haunting atmosphere). In this book, I have described how the cheesecloth/gauze in the puppet theatre wall divider may be used.

Script – The written text of the play as original to the playwright.

Segue – The music continues on to the next number or piece, without pause or interruption, but with some joiner written in. In this book try to have your pieces of music professionally edited or "linked" so that there is a continuous flow... e.g., for the Dance/Drama Sticks or the 3 Poses exercises especially.

Set – All the scenery, or combination of scenery and stage props which decorate a scene with the purpose of representing the SETTING.

Stretching an Actor – Challenging the actor to play something "out of their norm" or out of their comfort zone.

Tableau – A scene or "picture," presented by silent, unmoving actors. (Originally, these were developed in the Greek theater to show a violent act, as during those times any violence on stage was prohibited.)

Upstaging – Taking attention away from an actor who SHOULD be the focus of interest. (An example could be that you are making a fuss over a prop SL when the primary is speaking CS, centre stage. This would be a figurative example of you upstaging another. Literally, of course, it is standing UPSTAGE from the primaries, making THEM turn their backs to the audience in order to face you.)

Wings – The offstage areas just to the right and left of the set, divided by hung curtains or scenery flats, used as entrances but which conceal the backstage areas. (Thus, the expression "waiting in the wings.")

About the Expert

With her first on-stage appearance at age 4, her first leading role at age 11 and her professional stage roles culminating primarily in character parts in comedies, and for troupes catering to parties and murder mystery dinner theatres, Julie Johnson decided in 1997 that she would be well-suited to TEACH Drama to others. After graduating with a four-year specialist degree in teaching the Performing Arts, she moved to England to further work in both schools and theater. While mostly teaching high school Theater Arts since then (in three different countries) she has also been a leader of workshops for pre-teens and adults, a guest-speaker at college level, an adjudicator for theatre festivals and a coach and judge for speech and debate competitions. Here, in this guide, she offers many of her tips, games and exercises for teaching three different age groups under 18 years.

HowExpert publishes quick 'how to' guides on all topics from A to Z by everyday experts. Visit HowExpert.com to learn more.

Recommended Resources

- HowExpert.com – Quick 'How To' Guides on All Topics from A to Z by Everyday Experts.
- HowExpert.com/free – Free HowExpert Email Newsletter.
- HowExpert.com/books – HowExpert Books
- HowExpert.com/courses – HowExpert Courses
- HowExpert.com/clothing – HowExpert Clothing
- HowExpert.com/membership – HowExpert Membership Site
- HowExpert.com/affiliates – HowExpert Affiliate Program
- HowExpert.com/writers – Write About Your #1 Passion/Knowledge/Expertise & Become a HowExpert Author.
- HowExpert.com/resources – Additional HowExpert Recommended Resources
- YouTube.com/HowExpert – Subscribe to HowExpert YouTube.
- Instagram.com/HowExpert – Follow HowExpert on Instagram.
- Facebook.com/HowExpert – Follow HowExpert on Facebook.

Made in the USA
Las Vegas, NV
13 January 2024